To order additional copies of this book, contact:
Xlibris
1-888-795-4274
www.Xlibris.com
Orders@Xlibris.com

ISBN: Softcover   978-1-7960-7760-5
        EBook   978-1-7960-7759-9

Print information available on the last page

Rev. date: 02/14/2020

FOREWORD

As we travel through the journey called life, we have witnessed people often receiving or giving gifts for celebratory occasions. When attending a wedding celebration, a birthday party, graduation, or anniversary we will applaud the occasion with honoring the person(s) with a gift. The opportunity to present a person with a gift is endless. It is our delight to rejoice with those who rejoice. It is our hope the gift will bring an abundance of joy. It is our desire to share in a person's happiness. We understand the purpose of a gift is designed to bring unspeakable joy to all those we love. 15

We always take pleasure in embracing the characteristics of our God. We know He is the gift Giver. There are several scriptures in which he tells us Jesus is a gift. The bible declares Jesus as an indescribable gift (2 Corinthians 9:15, If you knew the gift of God, (John 4:10), and God gave His only begotten son to the world *as a gift (John 3:16). Jesus Christ was a gift to the world, he was given to us by God to bring us love, joy, peace and eternal life.*

The bible gives us an insight into the how God will bring a gift to the world. Each book within the bible will directly or indirectly outline an expression of God's gift within a person(s). The gifts from God will bring a light of hope and gifts from God are good.

God is no respect of person, therefore He gives all His children a gift. As each has received a gift, use it to serve one another (1 Peter 4:10), every perfect gift is from above (James 1:17), there are many gifts but the same spirit. (I Corinthians 12:4)

There will moments in our lives when we have to be reminded we are gifts. The daily activities of our lives, our busy careers and social media may cause our gifts to become dormant. There will also be others who do not recognize the gift within their soul.

Jesus came to give us life and life more abundantly. He came to help us maximize our potential and represent the kingdom of God. He came to help us recognize our gifts so that we may be a blessing to all those we love.

This book also is a love letter to those to remind us we are a gift to the world. Wendell Tillman reminds us that Jesus came to help us that we are a gift. A gift from above and we have been assigned a destiny. The book came to remind us to unwrap our gift to show the light and love of God on earth.

Kimberly Jones

Genesis 1;26-27

Then God Said, "Let us make human beings in our image, to be like us. They will reign over the fish in the sea, the birds in the sky, the livestock, all the wild animals on the earth, and the small animals that scurry along the ground." So God created human beings in his own image in the image of God he created them; male and female he created them.

I am a Gift from God

I Am Unique

There is no one like me

I am one of a kind

I am an original.

I have Destiny

I am Great

I have Purpose

I will fulfill my Purpose

I have Joy

Printed in the United States
By Bookmasters